SENSORY MOTOR
ACTIVITIES FOR
Early Development

D0026506

For Aloysius, Cara, Joe, Katrina, Rita, Raymond, Petrina, Sarah and Zachary

SENSORY MOTOR ACTIVITIES FOR
Early Development

**Chia Swee Hong
Helen Gabriel &
Cathy St John**

Illustrations by Sarah Avey

Speechmark Publishing Ltd
Telford Road, Bicester, Oxon OX26 4LQ, UK

Published by
Speechmark Publishing Ltd, Telford Road, Bicester, Oxon OX26 4LQ,
United Kingdom
Tel: +44 (0) 1869 244644   Fax: +44 (0) 1869 320040
www.speechmark.net

First published 1996
Reprinted 1998, 1999, 2000, 2002, 2004, 2005, 2006

© S H Chia, H Gabriel & C St John, 1996

Illustrations copyright © S Avey

All rights reserved. The whole of this work including all text and
illustrations is protected by copyright. No part of it may be copied,
altered, adapted or otherwise exploited in any way without express
prior permission, unless in accordance with the provisions of the
Copyright Designs and Patents Act 1988 or in order to photocopy or
make duplicating masters of those pages so indicated, without
alteration and including copyright notices, for the express purposes
of instruction and examination. No parts of this work may otherwise
be loaded, stored, manipulated, reproduced, or transmitted in any
form or by any means, electronic or mechanical, including
photocopying and recording, or by any information, storage and
retrieval system without prior written permission from the publisher,
on behalf of the copyright owner.

002-2285/Printed in the United Kingdom/1010

British Library Cataloguing in Publication Data
Chia, Swee Hong
    Sensory motor activities for early development
    1. Perceptual–motor processes
    I. Title   II. Gabriel, Helen   III. St John, Cathy
    155.4'12
ISBN 0 86388 418 0
ISBN 978 0 86388 418 4
(Previously published by Winslow Press under ISBN 0 86388 153 X)

Contents

Chia Swee Hong has extensive knowledge and experience in working with children and older people who have developmental disabilities such as learning difficulties, multiple learning disabilities and mental health difficulties in North London, Cheshire and Norfolk. He is currently a lecturer at the school of Occupational Therapy and Physiotherapy, University of East Anglia, Norwich, Norfolk. Swee is author and co-author of books including *Activities Digest*, *Living Skills for Mentally Handicapped People* and *Occupational Therapy in Childhood*.

Helen Gabriel has worked as a senior paediatric occupational therapist with children with disabilities for a number of years. She is a Bobath-trained therapist and has been based at the Royal Hampshire County Hospital, Winchester. Helen has spent a large proportion of her time working at Medcroft Opportunity Centre, a pre-school education centre for children with special needs in Winchester. She is the co-author of *GEMS – Guide to Early Movement Skills: A Portage-Based Programme*.

Cathy St John qualified as an occupational therapist in 1984 and began working in a residential unit for adults with a learning disability. Cathy worked in community occupational therapy and was involved in establishing and managing the first school-based occupational therapy service in Enfield. She has served as head OT with Enfield Community Health Care NHS Trust managing paediatric, wheelchair and GP unit OT services and continues to develop paediatric OT services within Enfield.

Acknowledgements

We have valued and benefited greatly from feedback about the structured programme of activities from parents, staff and children in the schools (in particular Chapel Road, Hall, Harford Manor and Springfield) we visit in Cheshire, Hampshire, North London and Norfolk. We would also like to thank our friends and colleagues, Rachel Barker, Judy Beare, Katherine Dyer, Victoria Cooper, Kim Sadler and Marianne Westwood for their constructive comments on the manuscript, colleagues at the Jenny Lind Child Development Unit, Norwich, for their resourceful ideas, Sue Christelow at Winslow for editorial support and Tracey Hourd for typing the manuscript.

For the sake of clarity alone, we have used 'he' to refer to the child with disabilities.

Introduction

As practitioners, we spend a considerable amount of time, together with carers, in assessing the needs of children and adolescents who have developmental delays or disabilities and devising activity programmes for them. Over the years we have developed, in collaboration with carers who are parents or practitioners, a package of tried and tested activities for developing gross and fine motor activities. We have used the activities to help children:

- **who do not initiate movement: for example, children with profound multiple learning disabilities;**
- **who have difficulties or require help with their movement: for example, children with cerebral palsy; and**
- **who need to refine their movement: for example, children who have dyspraxia.**

We have been influenced by reading and attending courses based on the works of Dr J Ayres, Dr K Bobath and Mrs B Bobath, Ms S Levitt, Ms F Longhorn, Mr G MacKay and Mr W Dunn, Mr J Presland and Mrs V Sherborne

If you notice that we have used your materials and neglected to give you credit, please accept our apologies and let us know.

Occasionally, this manual will mention the use of specialist equipment or splints — if these are required for your child, contact your therapist for advice, assessment and provision of these items.

We have not arranged the activities strictly according to age as we feel that this type of categorization should not be the priority. We have tended to select activities according to the 'needs' which have been commonly identified by carers. We are also aware that one activity can be used to develop many abilities: for example, a child who requires help with his

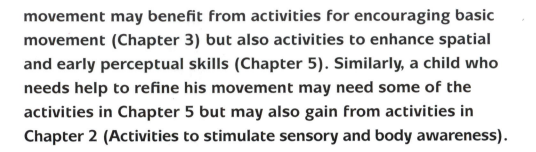

movement may benefit from activities for encouraging basic movement (Chapter 3) but also activities to enhance spatial and early perceptual skills (Chapter 5). Similarly, a child who needs help to refine his movement may need some of the activities in Chapter 5 but may also gain from activities in Chapter 2 (Activities to stimulate sensory and body awareness).

It is important for you to identify an aim (or aims), select an activity (or activities), break down the activity (or activities) and involve the child as much as possible in the 'whole' experience of carrying out the activity.

The activities are presented in a format which we hope is accessible to carers; any part of this manual can be photocopied to use as worksheets, for activity programmes, or as handouts for parents or other carers.

We hope the manual will help carers and, in particular, newly qualified practitioners who often ask the question: "Where do I begin?" and encourage them to work together in enabling their child to become more independent.

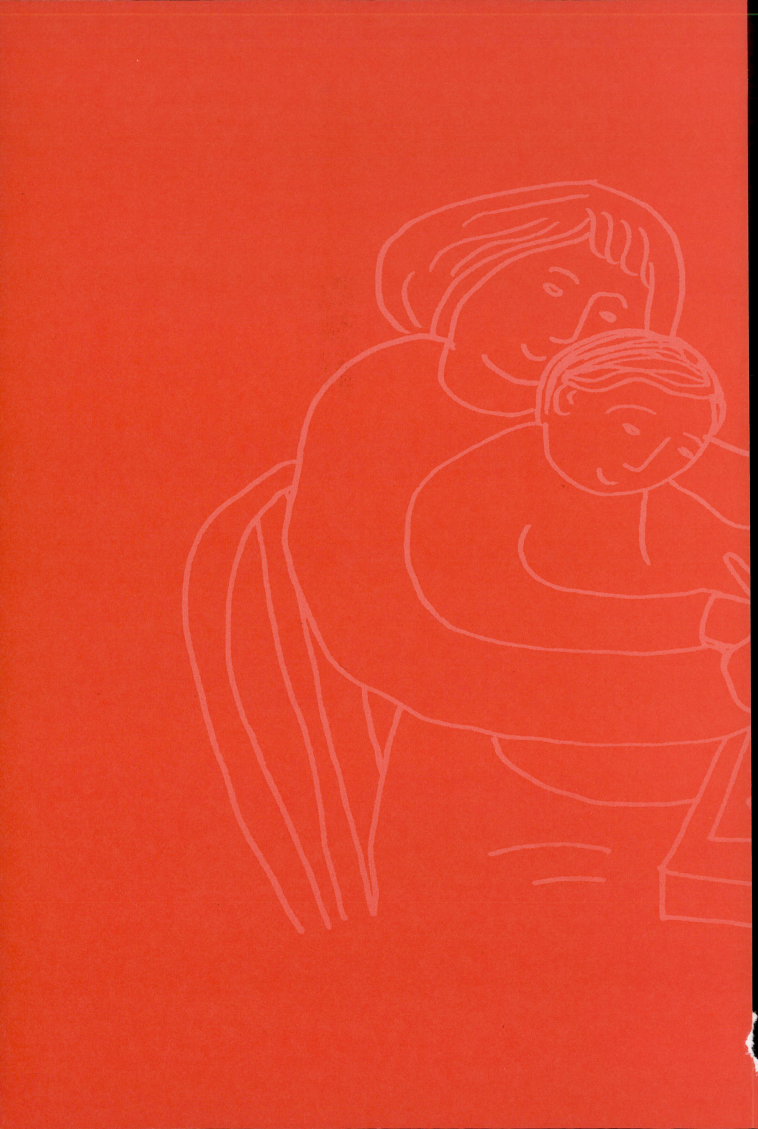

Getting started

You and your family are the child's best playthings. Your child will respond to care, attention and love and, with your help, your child can become more independent. We have given some general guidelines to help you to make your interaction with your child a positive one.

General Hints

- Fill your child's day — find lots of things for your child to look at, think about and do and make time for rest.

- Talk about everything you do.

- Share the responsibility for your child's care with others.

- Look for ways to turn activities into games. Find ways of enjoying each other's company and have fun together. If it is fun and interesting for your child, you are less likely to become tired and harassed.

- Find something that your child is good with and can be positive about. Use things which can be used to motivate the child.

- Never leave your child unsupervised. Make sure you use toys which conform to your country's safety standards.

- Make a collection of odds and ends such as boxes, bottle tops, scraps of materials, wrapping papers and dressing up clothes.

- Reduce the help you give as and when appropriate in activity sessions or in day-to-day activities.

- Ensure that everyone who works with and has contact with the child uses a consistent approach — provided it works!

- Join organizations such as local libraries or playgroups for children with special needs that can help and inspire you.

Before an activity session

- Create a happy and relaxed atmosphere, using appropriate rooms and minimizing distractions — movement, background music, television or toys cluttering the room.

- Be practical, be realistic. Choose skills and activities that will help the child to become more independent and able to do more for himself and others. If possible, plan activities to progress naturally from one skill to the next.

- Make sure you and your child are relaxed and that you have the time to work with him.
- Make sure you have all the equipment that is needed in the session.

During an activity session

- Try to be at the same level as your child, whether sitting on the floor or at the table. Ensure that your child feels happy and secure.
- If your child is unable to move, make sure he is appropriately placed — keep his head, trunk and limbs in a symmetrical position. Change this position frequently, as remaining static can lead to stiffness and deformities.
- Set short but regular sessions for one-to-one work. Introduce a new activity slowly and carefully. Give plenty of practice with any new skills.

- When beginning an activity, break the task down into small, manageable steps. Ensure that you have the child's attention before starting. Allow time for your child to respond.
- Talk to your child as you work with him and direct his attention. Encourage your child to initiate the movement.
- Be expressive. Use your face and the tone of your voice to show your feelings and thoughts.
- Praise your child: this will help him to develop his confidence and ability to learn new skills.
- Encourage your child to make choices and to take turns.
- Be firm and set guidelines and limits, but work alongside your child rather than lead.

After an activity session

- Observe your child. Try to understand what he thinks, what he knows and how he uses his new skills. *Keep records.*
- Display any new skills or pieces of work for others to admire.
- Make a space: for example, lie on the floor and allow time for doing nothing and being quiet from time to time.

Keep a profile of your child

Maintain a record of your child's achievements, a photographic record of your child and his favourite things, and update it. Put it in plastic flip folders so that your child can enjoy browsing through it. Ideas for content could include:

- A photo or a picture of your child drawn by himself
- My name is...
- My nickname is...
- I am...
- I live in...
- I live with...
- I like to play with...
- I like to eat...
- I like to drink...
- I like to wear...
- My favourite form of comfort is...
- My favourite story book is...
- My favourite shop is...
- My favourite programme is...
- My favourite pet is...
- My favourite place is...
- My biggest hate is...
- I am good at...
- I like to be able to learn to...

Development of movement and skills: a guideline

The following list gives an approximate idea of the age range in which most children gain certain skills. When using it as a guide, focus on the activity and not the age at which it was achieved.

Movement

Most children can:

- lift their head while lying on their belly (prone) by 3 months,
- sit with support by 6 months,
- play with feet by 6 months,
- roll over between 6 and 8 months,
- sit without support by 8 months,

- start trying to crawl around by 8 months,
- reach in all directions from sitting without falling over by 9 months,
- pull to standing position between 9 and 12 months,
- walk alone between 12 and 18 months,
- crawl upstairs by 12 months,
- kneel alone by 15 months,
- crawl (backwards) downstairs by 18 months,
- run well by 2 years,
- squat to play by 2 years,
- kick a ball by 3 years.

Hand—eye co-ordination

Most children can:
- look at a human face and watch a moving toy close to their face in first 2 months,
- look at their hands and bring hands together for finger play by 3 months,
- grasp briefly a rattle placed in their hand between 3 and 6 months,
- reach for toys with two hands, grasp and regard closely, by 4 to 6 months,
- pass toys from hand to hand by 6 months,
- reach with one hand by 7 months,
- release an object by pressing it on a hard surface by 9 months,
- begin to isolate the index finger and use a pincer grasp between 9 and 12 months,
- release toys deliberately, with increasing precision, between 9 and 12 months,
- finger feed and drink from a cup around 12 months,
- use fine pincer grasp, scribbling with a pencil (hand preference becoming obvious) by 2 years,
- throw a ball accurately by 2 years,
- undress, feed themselves and wash their hands by 3 years,
- draw a simple person and snip with scissors by 3 years.

Strategies

There are various techniques that can be used when teaching a new skill.

These include:

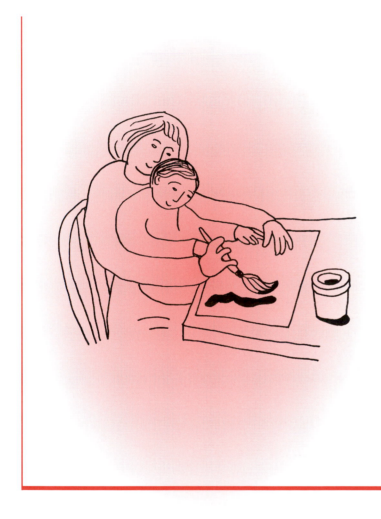

- Prompting, which could be *verbal* — telling the child what is wanted of him (for example, "Put the brick in the box"); *gestural* — indicating to the child what to do (for example, pointing from the brick to the box); or *physical* — guiding the child with your hands to carry out the activity (for example, holding the child's hand to help him grasp the brick or complete an activity such as painting a picture).

- Chaining, which involves breaking skills down into small steps which are taught either as forward chaining — the first step in the sequence is taught first — or as backward chaining — the last step in the sequence is taught first.

- Demonstrating, which is showing the child the idea of what the task looks like as it is going to be taught and/or what the finished product will look like.

- Fading, which is reducing the amount of help as the child begins to learn the new skill.

All of the above should make effective use of suitable toys, equipment and the environment and should incorporate any reinforcers which are likely to increase the child's motivation.

Breaking an activity down into small steps

A useful structure for breaking an activity down into small steps
is shown in the following example:

Name: *Tommy*

Activity: *Building a tower*

Aim: *To improve hand–eye co-ordination: Tommy has recently learned to build a tower of two bricks; he is now learning to build a tower with four bricks*

Equipment: *Four large wooden bricks*

Done by you	Done together	Done by Tommy
Gather equipment		
Gain child's attention		
Tell Tommy what you plan to do		
Place first brick on the table		*Place the second brick on top of the first one*
Ask Tommy to pick up third brick		*Pick up third brick*
	Place third brick on the tower	
Encourage Tommy to pick up fourth brick		*Pick up fourth brick*
	Place fourth brick on the tower	

Gradually reduce the help you give in placing the brick on the tower.

© Chia Swee Hong *et al* 1996
You may photocopy this page for instructional use only.

Observing and keeping records

This is a way of observing your child's performance:
Please tick the most appropriate number in each category.

Social interaction

1	2	3	4	5	6	7	8	9	10
☐	☐	☐	☐	☐	☐	☐	☐	☐	☐

Withdrawn – does not play or only rarely plays with others   *Interacts, shares and takes turns*

Attention

1	2	3	4	5	6	7	8	9	10
☐	☐	☐	☐	☐	☐	☐	☐	☐	☐

Is easily distracted from anything that he is doing   *Is able to ignore distractions and complete any activity*

Participation

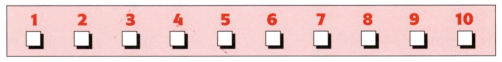

1	2	3	4	5	6	7	8	9	10
☐	☐	☐	☐	☐	☐	☐	☐	☐	☐

Constantly needs to be prompted   *Attempts new activity with confidence*

Co-operation

1	2	3	4	5	6	7	8	9	10
☐	☐	☐	☐	☐	☐	☐	☐	☐	☐

Finds it hard to keep still for any length of time   *Enjoys and participates actively*

Use a diary to keep a record of your child's reactions. Note how much help he needs to complete a task. Note any particular response to the activity:

Date	Activity	Response to the activity

You can also use videos, photos, a tape recorder, drawings and paintings.

© *Chia Swee Hong et al, 1996*
You may photocopy this page for instructional use only.

Questions to think about

When you are working with your child, you need to bear in mind the following questions:

- What do I want the child to do?
- What does the child want to do?
- What activities and equipment do I need?
- How can I break down each activity into small steps?
- How do I know that the child has learnt something?
- How can I encourage the child to transfer his learning skills?
- What are the next steps?

You may need extra support and guidance from appropriate professionals if your child has a challenging behaviour or difficulties in

- sitting or maintaining another posture,
- reaching for and grasping things,
- communicating his needs,
- responding to others.

Activities to stimulate sensory and body awareness

2

'Peekaboo, peekaboo, where are you?

Here I am, Here I am,

How do you do?'

Sensory and body awareness is crucial in order for children to be able to gain meaningful information from the environment. Information obtained in this way is interpreted at a sensory level. At this level, the child's basic senses, sight, hearing, smell, taste and touch, serve as channels through which this information can pass and identify individual stimulus. Consequently, we have initially to find activities to make the child aware of himself and his environment.

Activities to stimulate senses

Looking

- Use toys which are bright and colourful and which move easily: for example: mobiles, windmills, executive desk toys, fluorescent gloves, coloured mirrors, glitter paints, foil papers, fairy lights, a revolving mirror ball, bright mechanical toys, bubbles and balloons. Hang them, place them on the table or beside the child. Hold the toy and object between the child and mirror so the child has added visual input.

- Encourage the child to look at you while you put on a pair of colourful spectacles or a hat.

- Play peepbo games.

- Hold a torchlight about six inches in front of the child's face. Shine it across his face — not directly into it — or put a coloured washing liquid ball over the end of the torch. Gain his attention and gradually move the torch out to a distance of about one or two feet away. Encourage the child to follow the light as you move it horizontally, vertically or in different shapes. In a darkened room, shine a torch onto a fluorescent or shiny object.

- Blow bubbles and ask the child to watch and point as each bubble floats.

- Use face paints. Paint faces on your child and get him to paint on yours.

- Cut out a smiling face and a sad face in fluorescent paper or card or in black on white paper.

- Choose visual action songs and nursery rhymes, such as 'Incy Wincy Spider' or 'Two Little Dicky Birds Sitting on the Wall'.

- Talk and call the child's name. Encourage him to look towards you. Observe your child's responses in different lights, such as bright lights, dusky light or a dark room.

- Place easily grasped objects such as a wet sponge in his hand. Encourage him to discover any interesting features such as texture or temperature.

- Encourage the child to look at what is going on in the room, for example, fish swimming in the aquarium or cats having their dinner.

- Make food unusual. Colour it with food dyes.

- Arrange the food on his plate into interesting patterns, such as a face, or a train.

- When helping the child to dress, sit him in front of a mirror and encourage him to watch what he is doing.

- Use bath-time crayons: ask him to watch as you draw on his arms, hands and legs, then ask him to wash away the picture with a sponge.

Listening

- Use DIY plastic containers containing pasta or rice, rattles or commercially produced musical instruments (a Musical Instruments Box is available from Winslow) such as tambourines and cymbals, musical toys, squeakers, whoopee cushions and foreign music. Use loud noises as well as soft ones.

- Make a noise: for example, bang a drum. Encourage the child to turn towards the sound. Try a single note on a whistle, xylophone and so on, which may elicit more response than a continuous sound. Produce the sounds in as many ways as possible, such as loudly or quietly.

- Try with a variety of potential sound-making materials — dropping bricks into a container, sieving sand, pouring water from one container into another, tearing papers, tapping bottles containing various amounts of water, and so on.

- Sing a few nursery rhymes, such as 'I am the Music Man', or 'Old MacDonald had a Farm'. Include rhymes which involve movement; pause before the word associated with the movement and see if the child anticipates. For example, 'This is the way we brush our hair...'. Vary your voice in pitch and rhythm.

- Use the telephone and listen to the different tones.

- Make use of the daily routine: in the morning, turning on the tap, filling a mug of water, turning off the tap, squeezing toothpaste onto a brush, brushing teeth, rinsing and spitting out, and drying the mouth with a towel. Emphasize the sounds where possible.

- When in the kitchen, use various sizes of old saucepans and plastic containers and wooden spoons as drums and beaters.

Smelling

- Keep a box of materials with a distinctive smell such as *Jiffy* lemons, lavender bags, coffee grains, orange peel, aromatic soaps, perfume, pot-pourri, dried herbs, bath oil, spice bags and aftershave. Talk to the child about the smells and say: "You like that smell" or "You don't like that smell" as appropriate to his response.

- Have smelling games, for example guessing the above items.

- Use a variety of smells within cooking sessions: spices, pungent vegetables, cheese. Make herbal tea.

- Grow herbs in the garden. Dry them and put them in little sachets.

- Use everyday smells — from mowing grass, cutting the hedge or regularly used cooking ingredients — to see if the child recognizes them.

- Use massage oils when doing your child's stretches or for pleasure.

- Change the daily bath. Get some herbal bath oil beads or bubble bath and have a warm, relaxing bath.

- Play with a tray of pot-pourri.

Tasting

Collect the following:

- food and drink with hot tastes, such as curry powder and sauce, Worcestershire sauce and mustard sauce;

- food and drink with sweet tastes, such as chocolate spread, sorbets, honey and jam;

- food and drink with savoury tastes, such as brown sauce, cheese spread, *Marmite* and *Twiglets*;

- food and drink with salty tastes, such as salt, crisps, dried meat, anchovies and seafood.

- Use different textures, for example a range of common and exotic fruits.

- When tasting, give the child small portions of food and drink on his tongue, to avoid choking. Leave plenty of time between tastes to avoid flooding the taste sensation.

- Talk to the child, especially if he shows likes or dislikes of some tastes: for example, "You don't like the crusty bread" or "The smooth ice cream was nice".

Feeling

- Sing action rhymes and songs involving parts of the body: for example, 'This Little Piggy Went to Market' and 'Round and Round the Garden'.

- Hold toys which vary in texture, such as a spiky brush and a soft teddy bear, one at a time.

- Ask your child to feel or identify materials which are:
  soft — cotton wool, crepe paper, sand, handcream, feathers, fur fabric;
  hard — spoons, bricks, pasta, large beach pebbles;

rough — pot scourers, sandpaper, hooks of *Velcro*, hairbrush;
smooth — glass, a piece of silk;
pliable — *Playdough*, sponges, balloons;
light — paper, ping-pong ball;
heavy — a piece of iron.

• Collect in a box an assortment of real or pictured objects that can be easily grouped as things to feel (feather, sandpaper), to smell (perfumed towel, flower), to hear (whistle, picture of a guitar) and to taste (pictures of food). Label four paper bags with pictures to represent the four senses and ask the child to sort the objects and place each one in its appropriate bag.

• Do foot and finger painting with materials such as sand, corn or starch mixed with paint.

• Draw a design or a letter on a carpet sample with chalk. Ask the child to identify them and then erase them with a towel.

• Play 'tick–tack–toe' with carpet samples. Erase chalk marks with arms and hands.

• Prepare stencil cut-outs of shapes, such as a circle, square, diamond, triangle or rectangle, letters and numerals. Encourage the child to feel the shapes and use the stencil to draw it.

• Make a tactile collage using a variety of fabrics, papers or leaves. Hang the collage where the child can touch it as he walks past.

• Ask the child to place his hands under a pillow. You gently pull on one finger and the child guesses which finger was pulled.

• Roll up the child in a big towel or blanket into a Swiss roll or sausage. Roll him and pat him to put on icing sugar or stroke him to put on sauce.

• Lay your child, wearing few clothes, on different textures, such as sheepskin, grass, a thermal blanket and bubble plastic. Roll your child along this surface and, if appropriate, encourage him to crawl or walk along it.

• Ask him to lie on his back and smooth him with the flat of your hands, using body cream. Blow raspberries on his feet, hands, back, belly and face.

• When the child is having his regular bath, pour warm water over his shoulders, back and belly. When he is being dried, let him help you rub over him. Put talcum powder or lotions onto his body.

Activities to enhance body awareness

- Shine a flashlight on to various parts of the child's body and ask him to tell you where the torch is shining.

- Trace the body outline of the child and ask him to draw in the parts.

- Use 'body parts' jigsaw puzzles.

- Help your child to cut up a picture of a body into major parts and then paste it together again.

- Encourage your child to play with 'Potato Face' and arrange the features appropriately.

- Let your child look into a mirror while dressing or when performing various classroom activities. Extend this by encouraging him to look at and copy body positions or facial expressions in the mirror.

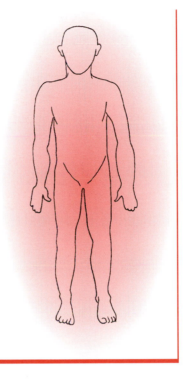

- Play 'back to back' with an uneven number of children. Ask each to stand back-to-back with a partner. The child without a partner should give directions, such as elbow to elbow or nose to nose, which the other children should follow. Then all change partners, with a new child giving the directions.

- Sing 'Head, Shoulders, Knees and Toes' and 'If You are Happy and You Know it'.

- Play 'Simon says...'.

- Play with a 'Twister'.

- At bath time, name body parts and rub them with different textures, such as a sponge, loofah, nail brush or talcum powder.

Activities to promote awareness of hands

- Blow raspberries on the child's hands — on the palms and the backs of his hands and on the fingers.

- Rub his hands with different textures, for example fur fabric, bubble wrap, rough towelling.

- Play with his hands, tickling his palms and putting them on your cheeks.
- Attach bells or rattles to his wrists: as he moves his hands they will make a noise.
- Draw faces on the palms and the backs of his hands.
- Place thimbles on his fingertips.

- Place an object in the child's hand or close to him so that he can feel, grasp or explore it.
- Encourage handling and playing with hard and soft play materials.
- Play finger games, such as 'Incy Wincy Spider' and 'Two Little Dicky Birds Sitting on the Wall'.

- Encourage the child in messy play — use sand, water, *Playdough*, shaving foam and cornflour paste.
- Paint his hands and ask him to paint his own hands.
- Encourage him to place his hands in a plastic container containing rice, lentils, polystyrene chips and/or soapy water.
- Use finger puppets made with bright textured fabrics.

Activities to develop awareness of object permanence (that things continue to exist, even though they can no longer be seen)

- Roll a ball along a level surface and encourage your child to follow the ball with his eyes. Place a box in the path of the ball. Roll the ball in and then let it out.

- Cover your head with a scarf. Lift it up and smile and greet the child or play 'peepbo'.
- Partially cover a favourite toy with a scarf or a towel and ask your child to 'find' it. As this skill develops, cover the toy completely.
- Drop a toy through a short tube so that it makes a noise when it emerges. Gradually lengthen the tube, and then seal off the bottom of it so your child needs to empty it to retrieve the toys. Use musical toys at first, such as balls with bells in.

- Hide toys in boxes and ask your child to find them.
- Use everyday toys. Push a train into a tunnel; drive a car into a garage; push Jack into the box and let him jump up again.
- Play hide and seek with other children and adults.

Activities to encourage awareness of cause and effect

Through play, your child can learn that a specific action will trigger a response. Keep a collection of toys and equipment which will move or react the instant they are moved or struck: for example, a drum will bang, a balloon will squeak, a mobile will sway or a ball will roll.

- Use 'pull-along' toys, such as caterpillars.
- Use toys which produce a visual effect, such as kaleidoscopes and light sticks that glow in the dark.
- Play with sound makers, such as rattles, squeaky toys, an electronic organ, crumpled papers and 'groan tubes', which make a noise when moved.
- Choose toys that open and close, such as a Jack-in-the-Box, doors and keys.
- Choose toys that fit together, such as nesting boxes or inset boxes or pop-up stacking toys.
- Build a tower of bricks and knock them down.
- Use switches: pressing the switch will make the toys move or make appropriate computer programmes such as a touch screen work.

Activities for encouraging basic movement

3

'Row, row, row your boat,

Gently down the stream,

Merrily, merrily, merrily, merrily,

Life is but a dream.'

From birth onwards, as the central nervous system matures, movement patterns gradually develop from the reflex actions of the infant into the great variety of movement of an adult. By maturity these reflexes reach such a degree of refinement that it is possible to maintain body posture, that is balancing head, trunk and legs, while the arms are involved in manipulative activities.

Children who have disabilities such as cerebral palsy need to be handled and positioned appropriately in order to help their physical development, minimize the influence of abnormal reflexes and prevent problems such as deformities.

Basic positions

Ideally, keep the child's head in midline (looking forwards). The trunk and limbs should be even (symmetrical) and kept straight (extended), with both arms in front of his body to enable him to use his hands where he can see them. The child should bear weight equally through hips, knees and feet and try to minimize abnormal bending of any part of the body towards the back or front.

When carrying the child who has stiffness (spasticity), carry him astride your hips, keeping the child's hips and knees bent, knees well apart, his arms forward at the shoulders.

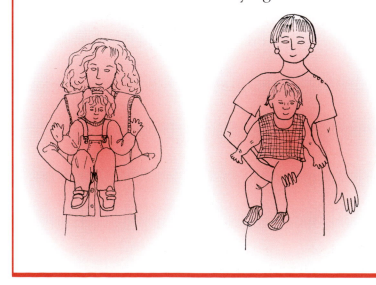

When carrying the child who is floppy, hold him securely around the pelvis with his hips and knees bent, as in a sitting position. The child's head is unsupported but in this position, he is encouraged to lift his head up.

When carrying the child who has involuntary movement (athetosis), hold him firmly, keeping his arms forward and his knees and hips bent. The child can now concentrate on moving his head independently and can learn to look around.

Positions and related activities

Lying on the back

This is usually the least useful position for a child to be in. When on his back, it is difficult for him both to look at toys and to play with them.

- Place your child on a foam wedge or a firm cushion. The slight incline will give him a better view of his surroundings. If necessary, a roll made of foam can be placed between the legs just above the knees to help to keep them apart.

- Encourage your child to lie symmetrically on his back. His legs should be straight and apart, arms down by his sides or together in midline and his head in the middle while you talk and sing with him.

- Placing the child in a hammock may help to keep his head and shoulders forward.

- Help him to explore and to be aware of different parts of his body (for example, rub cream on his legs and feet).

- Encourage the child to clap his hands or do finger rhymes, such as 'Incy Wincy Spider' or 'Pat-a-Cake'.

- Give your child a torch and help him to hit targets with the beam of light.

- Gently move your child's limbs through the normal range of movement: bend and straighten his elbows, hold his feet and bend his hips and knees. Clap the soles of his feet.

- Bend his knees up to his chest. Gently lean over him. Take his hands and encourage him to feel your face or necklace.

- With his knees bent, hold your child's feet flat on the floor. Ask him to raise his bottom to let the train under the bridge.

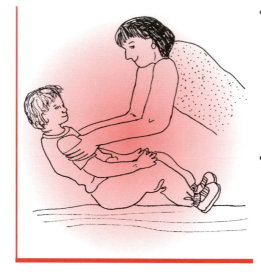

- To help him develop head control, hold his shoulders and pull him up gently until his head hangs back a little, then lay him down again. Do it often and, as he gains control, lift him a little higher.

- Using a frame of toys positioned over your child, encourage him to turn his head and then keep it in the middle for a short time as he looks at the toys.

- Further develop head control by providing stimulus for the child to turn his head to one side, back to the middle, to the other side and back to the middle again by talking, singing or using motivating toys.

- Bring both the child's hands up towards your face before you pick him up.

Lying on the side

This is a good position to encourage the child to see and use both hands together in front of the body. It is also a good preparatory step towards rolling.

- When positioning your child on his side first encourage him to turn his head to one side, say to the right. Gently bend his left knee and lift it over the right from the hip. Place his left arm across his chest and gently push him over to his right side.

- When the child is lying on his side, place a rolled up towel or pillow behind him to help him maintain the position. Alternatively, lay him along the back of the seat of a sofa. Make sure he does not fall off from the sofa.

- If necessary, use a side-lying board, a piece of equipment which secures and supports the child in a comfortable side-lying position.

- Place your child on an inflatable mattress. Press the mattress to one side of his body so that he tips and rolls.

- When your child is lying on his back, bend one hip and knee well over to the opposite side and wait for him to complete the roll. Place musical toys on either side of him and ask him to turn to look at them.

- Teach your child to roll from his belly onto his back, one side at a time. For example, when rolling from the right side, the child should lie on the floor or other firm surface as usual. Encourage him to lift his head up and turn to the left and ask him to keep his right arm up above his head. Control the rolling movement by placing one hand behind his head and the other just above the knee of his left leg.

- Play games involving rolling from side to side, picking toys up at one side and transferring them from hand to hand before rolling to the other side and placing them in a container, for example putting shapes into a post box.

Lying on the belly

Lying on his belly will encourage and help the child to hold his head up, to straighten his trunk, take the weight through his elbows and stretch his hips.

- Use a roll, pillow or wedge, or lay the child across your legs. Ensure that there is room for his toes to drop down at the end of the wedge. This will keep his ankles in a good position. The front of the wedge should be of a suitable depth to enable the child to support himself on his elbows. His forearms should be away from his body with elbows at right angles to the trunk — ideally his hands should be open. Ensure that his head and trunk are symmetrical and straight, with legs apart and turned out at the hips.

- Place your child over a large roll or a beach ball and rock him backwards and forwards. Alternatively, try a water bed, inflatable bed or hold him over your lap.

- If your child does not like lying on his belly, try placing him on your chest when you lie on the floor or the bed. Talk, sing and hold him close so he feels secure.

- Lay your child over your legs when you sit on the floor with legs outstretched. Your legs will give him support under his chest and will help him take his weight through his forearms or, later, through straight arms and flat hands.

- Place the child on hands and knees over a towel and, when he is comfortable, encourage him to crawl.

Sitting

This is a useful position for self-care, play and school work. It enables the child to be in better contact with the environment, encourages extension of the spine, improves head control and frees the hands for play. When seating a child, consider the following points:

1 the child's bottom should be well back in the chair,

2 his weight should be equally distributed through buttocks and thighs,

3 his head and back should be held erect and in the midline,

4 his trunk should be leaning slightly forwards,

5 his hips, knees and ankles should be flexed at right angles,

6 both feet should be flat on the floor (or on an appropriate foot box) to maintain the hip, knee and ankle positions,

7 a large table or a tray with a single, horizontal pole that the child can grasp at arm's length may help him to maintain stability through trunk and shoulder girdle and therefore improve head control.

• Introduce your child to a chair even if he needs full support.

• Sit on a chair with your child on your knee with a table at chest height, and his arms supported on this. Support him fully with your body then gradually reduce the support, for example, holding him around the shoulders as he gains more trunk control.

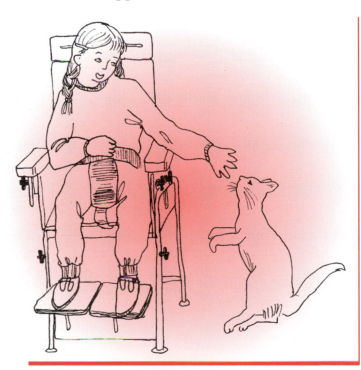

• When the child is sitting up from lying on the floor, place your hands firmly on the outside of his shoulders and slowly and gently lift him upwards into a sitting position, giving him plenty of time to respond to the movement. Support his shoulders while you encourage him to sit up, lifting up at a diagonal. Gently move him back down to lying — repeat several times. Encourage him to keep his chin in to his chest.

- If your child is attempting to lift his head when you pull him up to a sitting position, pull him up to this position holding both his elbows instead of his shoulders. Later, you can help him to keep one hand down on the floor and he can lower himself down to lying.

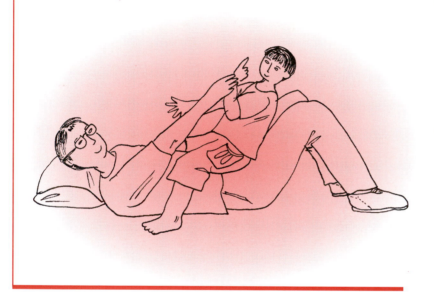

- Sit your child between your legs on the floor so he has support behind him and to the sides. Gradually remove the support as he becomes more stable.

- When your child is used to sitting on the floor with this support, gradually reduce the support you give him until he is sitting for a few moments on his own. When he is confident, encourage him to raise one hand off the floor.

- Encourage your child to prop himself with straight arms and hands in front, when he is supported at the back and sides. As you remove support, encourage propping at the sides. For example, sing 'Seesaw, Marjorie Daw' as you tilt him gently from side to side to take his weight through straight arms and flat hands, if possible.

- Encourage side sitting — help your child to sit on one hip with legs curled round to the side, propping himself on the opposite arm and playing with the free hand.

- Encourage regular movement between sitting, side sitting and hands and knees.

- Encourage your child to sit when reading, doing puzzles and so on. When the child is sitting, surround him with toys so he has to reach and stretch to pick them up. Make sure the child is given the opportunity to sit on a regular chair, on a stool or any other chairs.

Standing

Standing contributes to the stability of the child's hips and knee joints and provides a different range of visual, sensory and social experiences. A good standing position is with feet flat on the floor and the weight going through slightly flexed hips and knees to the heels and feet.

- When your child is in a crawling position, place his hands on a low, stable chair. Position his feet correctly and encourage him to push himself up into a supported standing position by half-kneeling.

- Sit on a chair with your knees bent at ninety degrees. Support the child in a standing position between your thighs.

- Kneel down, sitting on your heels and sit the child on your knee. Place your hands on his knees and, as you rise to an upright kneeling position, press downwards on his knees to bring him to a standing position.

- Stand to play at the sofa or a low table. Place toys gradually further away so your child has to move slightly to reach them.

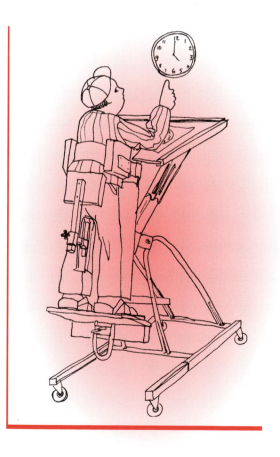

- Encourage your child to lean less on the sofa as his balance improves. Encourage him to shift his weight from leg to leg.

- Use wall bars (or a suitable sturdy chair). Place the child's hands on a bar level with the height of his shoulders while he is kneeling. As he stands up through half-kneeling, encourage him to raise his hands up the bars.

- When he is standing, make sure the child's feet are flat on the floor and his weight is equally distributed. His legs should be slightly bent at the hips and knees, a little apart and slightly outwards (externally rotated) with the trunk upright.

- If your child is not able to stand, consult your therapist, who may suggest a prone board or a standing frame.

Walking

- Place attractive toys at one end of a sofa or table. Help your child side-step to reach them.

- Stand or kneel behind the child, who is standing, with your hands on the outside of his hips. Gently sway the child's body from side to side so that his body weight is being transferred from one leg to the other.

- Stand your child with one leg slightly in front of the other and practise the same exercise, transferring weight forwards and backwards as the child sways.

- Combine the above two exercises and prompt the child to move one leg forward as he sways, then to transfer the weight on to that leg.

- Walk with variations in:

  speed and step size — use hoops for him to step into and out of; use newspaper islands;

  parts of the foot used — heel—toe—outside—inside;

  direction— forwards, backwards and sideways.

Activities to promote hand skills

4

'Tommy Thumb, Tommy Thumb,

Where are you?

Here I am, here I am,

How do you do?

Peter Pointer...

Toby Tall...

Ruby Ring...

Baby Small...

Fingers all, Fingers all...'

Hand function depends, not only on the physical control of the trunk, shoulder, arms and hands, but also on visual, perceptual and cognitive development. Hand function consists of reach, grasp and release, and competence in the use of the hand is required for supporting the body weight, for moving into different positions, for grasping, manipulating, feeling and communicating.

Before beginning activities for hand skills, if sitting on a chair, check that:

- the child's knees and hips are at right angles when in weight-bearing positions;

- his shoulders and arms are turned out from the body rather than in towards the body;

- his hands are open with palms down if he is bearing weight through them.

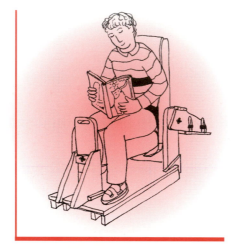

Position the child where he is free to use his hands. If necessary:

• elbow splints can be used to maintain straight elbows when the child is taking weight through his hands;

• open the child's hands by placing the heels of his hands against a firm surface.

Activities to encourage specific hand skills

Reaching

- Use objects which will encourage the child to reach, such as mobiles (commercial or home-made), faces, bright clothes, jewellery, leaves on trees, wobbly toys, a bumble ball (a battery-operated ball which vibrates), balloons and bubbles.

- Encourage him to pull a cord which activates a musical box or a puppet.

- Have a tug of war.

Grasping with the whole hand (palmar grasp)

- Use rattles, 'groan tubes' (a tube which makes a noise when moved), tinsel sticks, squeaky toys.

- Encourage the child to take objects from and put objects back into a container.

- Squeeze squeakers, sponges or *Playdough*.

Releasing objects

- Ask the child to drop objects into a large container; use smaller containers as he develops the skill.

- Use posting boxes and shape sorters.

- Make patterns with large and small pegs on a board.

- Throw bean bags onto a target or into a bucket.

- Play dominoes.

- Have a game of 'Pass the Parcel'.

Using a flat hand

- Encourage the child to bear weight through his hands by crawling or walking 'on all fours'.

- Play 'Pat-a-Cake' or other clapping games.

- Make handprints in paint, sand or *Playdough*.
- Visit a farm or children's zoo, where the child can stroke the animals or feed them treats from flat hands.

Transferring an object from one hand to the other

- Use toys which require manipulation to explore, such as *Koosh* animals (animal-like balls), made from thin strands of rubber.
- Play games on the floor, with the child rolling to one side to pick something up, transferring it to the other hand when lying on his back, then rolling to the other side to place the toy in a container, a man in a car, and so on.

Using a fist

- Sing action songs, such as 'Peter bangs with one hammer...'.
- Encourage the child to pull or hammer pegs.
- Encourage the child to hold and carry a cup.
- Ask him to hold the brush and brush his hair.

Grasping with the thumb, and middle finger (tripod grasp)

- Encourage the child to post cylindrical shapes or pick up and use pencils and crayons.
- Paint or paste some pictures using a fat paintbrush.

Grasping with a thumb and finger ends (pincer grasp)

- Use pegs, beads, buttons, toys on a string, puzzles with knobs.
- The child clips pegs onto his clothes and removes them.

Using index finger with other fingers

- Use toys that need a knob to activate them, such as a telephone, or a pop-up cone tree or Humpty Dumpty toys, that have to be pressed.
- Play pointing games.
- Encourage the child to use his fingers to make holes in *Playdough*.
- Play the piano.

- Play games with finger puppets.
- Sing and play finger rhymes.

Using the thumb

- Do thumb or finger prints.
- Make pictures by pushing drawing pins into a board.
- Ask the child to use his thumb to cover up faces or stickers on his finger pads.
- Press studs on clothes or home-made rag books.

General ideas to promote hand use

- Play threading games with cotton reels, buttons and cards.
- Make a collage, encouraging cutting, sticking and pasting.
- Encourage the child to attempt all types of fastenings when he is getting dressed.
- Give the child small snacks in narrow containers and encourage him to use finger and thumb in opposition to reach the snack.
- Present his packed lunch in a number of different containers: for example, the main carrier has a zip fastening, some have screw tops, others snap-top lids, and so on.
- Ask your child to help in the kitchen — he can hold the bowl while someone else mixes, sift the flour, use a rolling pin, and so on.
- When bathing the child, encourage him to apply soap to sponge and rub it on his body.

Activities to enhance spatial and early perceptual skills

5

'One finger, one thumb, keep moving
One finger, one thumb, keep moving
One finger, one thumb, keep moving
We all be merry and bright!

One finger, one thumb and one arm, keep moving
One finger, one thumb and one arm, keep moving
One finger, one thumb and one arm, keep moving
We all be merry and bright!

One finger, one thumb, one arm and one leg, keep moving
One finger, one thumb, one arm and one leg, keep moving
One finger, one thumb, one arm and one leg, keep moving
We all be merry and bright!'

As the child moves, sense organs in the ear identify the degree of movement that the body is experiencing and, if necessary, allow the body to take appropriate action. Experience in coping with changes in balance comes through movement, and if children are unable to move they may have limited experience of this and consequently of spatial awareness. Spatial awareness is the child's knowledge of his own position and his relationship to objects in space, such as whether one object is on top of another or inside it.

Similarly, a child learns about the world through sensory and movement experience; the process of extracting information from sensory input is called perception. Perception, however, also makes use of past experience and present needs and enables the children to form concepts. Perception is the process of interpreting the patterns of sensory stimuli that each child receives.

It is easier for a child to retain and remember visual details if classification and discrimination have already been learned (visual memory). It is also helpful if the child is able to attach a verbal label to the various parts of a learning process. A related ability is closure, the ability to perceive and imagine missing parts.

In order to gain visual information the child has to learn to make logical sequences in a task and to co-ordinate a series of discrete fixations into a useful skill, such as learning left to right tracking before reading (sequencing and scanning). An establishment of left or right dominance and overall awareness of left and right seem to play a role here. Children have also to learn to make visual judgements about objects, for example regarding similarities and differences (visual discrimination).

Spatial activities

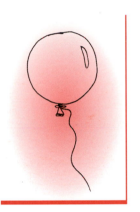

- Your child could use a scooter board to move around the room.
- Play with balloons — the child hits a balloon into the air, trying not to let it fall to the floor.
- Pretend to jump over puddles, (for example, using hoops on the floor); increase and decrease the size of the puddles.
- Ask your child to hit a suspended ball, first with his hand and then with a bat.
- Follow straight or zig-zag lines, first walking, then hopping. Later, try this wearing unusual shoes, such as shoe boxes, flippers, snow shoes, skis.
- Pretend to be animals and try out their methods of movement: a snake's wriggle, a bunny hop, elephant walk, and so on.
- While your child is lying on the floor, encourage him to make different shapes with his body, such as letters or numbers.
- Use a scooter board to knock over skittles.
- Make patterns and designs using small shapes.
- Use large apparatus toys, such as a bouncy castle, a ball pool or a climbing frame.
- Play ball games.
- Make an obstacle course using ropes, boxes, furniture and so on. Include actions which require the child to go over, beside, under, around and through obstacles, backwards and forwards.

- Play 'Angels in the Snow': the child lies on the floor and, using his arms and legs, copies the patterns demonstrated to him. This can be great fun when done at high speed.
- Have a simple treasure hunt, asking your child to follow directions on a map.
- Use inflatable toys, such as an air bed, or a bouncy castle.

Visual discrimination

- Encourage your child to sort out objects or things such as socks or plates by colour, type and shape.

- Ask the child to match three separate shapes with the same shapes represented on a piece of card.

- Hide bricks around the room and ask your child to find all of the red ones.

- Ask your child to find a small object hidden within a picture, as with 'Where is the owl?'.

- Encourage the child to copy line patterns on a dot grid, progressing from simple shapes to complex patterns.

- Draw a series of straight lines and ask the child to copy each shape using little sticks, for example to draw a house.

- Match similar pictures and words.

- Collect several tins of different sizes, each one with a lid. Take the lids off and mix them up. The child has to put the right lid back on the right tin.

- Line up a row of books of different heights on a table. The child has to arrange them in order of height.

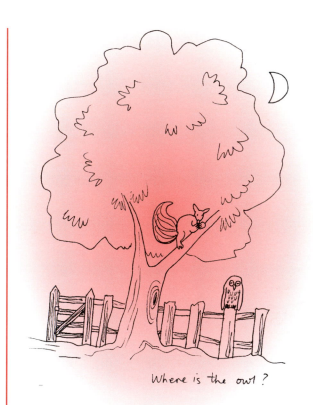

Where is the owl?

- Cut a piece of fruit in half and point out how the halves match in shape. Use them to print.

- Figures 1 to 7 present activities to help with visual discrimination.

Figure 1 *How many creatures can you find in Noah's ark?*

Figure 2 *Who is holding which balloon?*

Figure 3 *Which two fish are most alike?*

Figure 4 *Which house is different?*

Figure 5 *Which is the odd one out?*

Figure 6 *Which is the missing piece of apple?*

Figure 7 *Spot the difference — there are six changes*

Sequencing and scanning

- Clap your hands and ask the child to reproduce the sequence.
- Practise copying gross motor sequences: for example, clap hands, stamp feet, tap knees.
- Encourage fine motor sequences: oppose thumb to each finger in turn. Point to each finger in turn with the index finger of the opposite hand. Try to do it more quickly.
- Help your child to make a row of cars, bricks and so on, left to right, and put them away, left to right.

- Use a pegboard and ask the child to place pegs in a line left to right. Use pegs of one colour at first, then do a simple two-colour sequence, such as red, yellow, red, for the child to copy.

- Ask the child to carry on a sequence of dots, for example from left to right, and draw them in later.

- Show a series of picture cards in a set order, for example a car, a house, a cat, shuffle them and then ask the child to arrange them in the same order on the table, working from left to right.

- Practise visual sequences: for example, using coloured beads, copy a pattern when threading; or use old buttons and make a sequence for the child to copy.

- Practise auditory sequences — repeating a sequence of numbers, notes on the piano, and so on.

- Try playing with 'Simon', an electronic game involving visual and auditory sequencing.

Activities to encourage visual memory

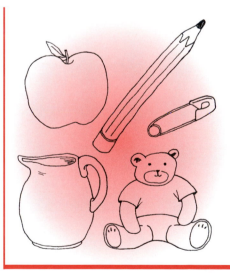

- Ask a group of children to stand in a circle; choose one child to study the rest of the group and then leave the room. Another child from the circle then hides and when the first child returns he has to say who is missing.

- Play Kim's game: place two or three objects on a tray, look at them and name them for a minute then cover them up and ask the child to remember what was on the tray. Gradually increase the number of objects as the child improves.

- Look at a picture for a few minutes, then hide it and ask your child questions about it: for example, "What colour is the ball?".

- Use a series of pictures, each of which has hidden objects. Ask the child to find and identify them.

- Encourage your child to practise drawing lines, shapes or figures from other drawings or pictures.

- For a child who can write, practise copying a sentence from one written on the same sheet of paper, then from another piece of paper propped up in front of him, then stuck on a wall further away.

Hand—eye co-ordination

- Draw parallel lines of varying widths on a piece of paper and ask your child to draw a line from left to right between the parallel lines, without touching them. Use pictures at each end of the parallel lines so the pencil has a journey: for example, take the mouse to the cheese.

- Present a simple dot pattern to the child and ask him to join the dots together into a given design.

- Draw various shapes on paper and ask the child to cut closely around each shape, cutting parallel to the lines drawn.

- Suspend a large ball from a door frame. Encourage the child to hit it with his hand, then with a bat. Progress onto a smaller ball.

- Play with a balloon: ask the child to hit it with his hand and try not to let it touch the ground.

- Use shaving foam or finger paints on a mirror or table with a big piece of plastic over it. Draw shapes with your index finger. Encourage the child to copy. Practise lines and circles.

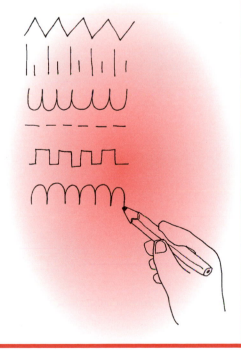

- When painting with a brush, encourage your child to paint lines from top to bottom and left to right and circular shapes when 'drawing'.

- When the child begins holding a fat crayon, make sure his thumb is uppermost if he is holding the crayon in a palmar grasp.

- Use big sheets of paper stuck to the wall or spread on the floor for *big* movements. Encourage the child to use his thumb, index and middle finger — a tripod grasp. Try with different crayons, pencils, paints and felt-tips. Encourage the child to copy patterns.

- Figures 8 to 12 involve more activities to do with the use of hand—eye co-ordination.

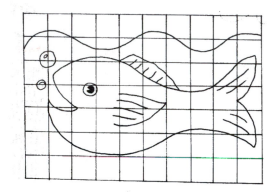

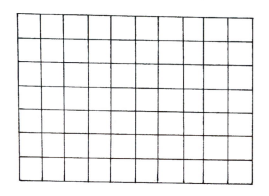

Figure 8 *Copy this picture in the squares*

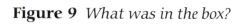

Figure 9 *What was in the box?*

Figure 10 *Complete the picture*

Figure 11 *Shade the dotted areas*

Figure 12 *Make two giraffes*

Directionality activities

- Ask the child to match feet, hands and knees with cut-out patterns of the same. Patterns can be laid out so that the child walks forward, jumps, hops or walks backwards.

- Place various coloured blocks on a desk. Move one block so it is nearer, on, under or away from the others and have the child describe its position.

- Have the child tell you the direction of certain letters (d, b, p) and objects (fish swimming, kite flying).

- Teach north, south, east, west by locating and marking sides of the room. Give the child a direction sheet which describes a route: for example, go north to the clock, three steps to the east and west to the door. Hide a prize at the end of the route.

Left and right discrimination

- Use wristbands of different colours or labelled 'left' and 'right'.

- Trace several copies of the child's left and right hand on a piece of cardboard. Pin them on a bulletin board where the child can match his hands to the patterns. Label each pattern left and right, as appropriate.

- Ask the child to name objects on his left, then on his right. Have him turn around 180 degrees and do the same.

- Ask which hand is holding the kite (see Figure 13).

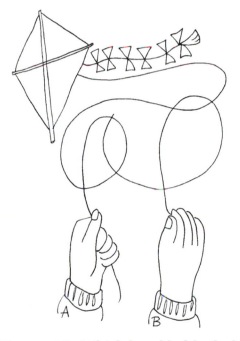

Figure 13 *Which hand holds the kite?*

- Use the left and right in everyday classroom activities. Have children stand to the right of their chairs. Ask girls to put their snacks on the right side of their juice, boys on the left side of their juice, and so on.

- Play opposite commands: instruct the child to respond by doing the opposite of what he is told to do. For example, when told to raise his right hand, he raises his left.

Working in small groups

6

> *'I'm a little teapot, short and stout,*
>
> *Here's my handle, here's my spout,*
>
> *When I see the tea-cups, hear me shout,*
>
> *Tip me up and pour me out.'*

Most of the techniques and ideas discussed in previous chapters have described working with a child individually. While invaluable benefits are gained from a one-to-one setting, it is equally important for children to play and experience situations alongside their peers, generalizing the skills they have gained from their individual work.

This chapter, though by no means providing an exhaustive list, consists of numerous activities which are an extension of earlier ideas and sets the scene for themes and structures which are most suited to small groups, ideally with one adult for every one or two children.

The overall aims for this type of group are to maintain or develop each child's ability to:

- relate and communicate with others and work as a group;
- develop awareness of themselves and their environment, attention and co-ordination;
- acquire some of the basic skills such as eye contact, sitting and reaching for and grasping toys and equipment, and using them;
- enjoy and gain confidence and achievement from tackling challenges;
- enhance creativity;
- identify further his strengths.

You may need to identify specific aims for a group you are involved with; for example:

- stimulate each child's hearing, sight, sense of touch, movement, smell and taste;

- encourage him to watch and play with toys and games;

- help him to be aware of cause and effect;

and to select activities to achieve those aims.

SESSION 1

Aim:

Stimulating sensory and body awareness

Activity:

Simple massage

Materials:

Hand cream

Opening the session

- Greet the children and introduce the activity. Encourage them to smell some hand cream.

Developing the session

- Hold the child's hand in your left or right hand, stroke lightly from the shoulder to the wrist, then firmly back up to the shoulder, first on the outside and then on the inside of the arm.
- Let go of the arm. Use both hands to squeeze gently the flesh of the upper arm.
- Stroke down the arm and over the hand.
- Grasp each finger between thumb and forefinger and pull from the joint to the fingertip, working the knuckles as you stroke over them.
- Stroke the whole hand several times.

Closing the session

- Encourage all the children to lie down and have a rest.

© Chia Swee Hong *et al* 1996
You may photocopy this page for instructional use only.

SESSION 2

Aim:

Stimulating sensory and body awareness

Activity:

Body awareness 1

Materials:

Large sheets of paper, pencils, scissors, paints

Opening the session

• Say hello and introduce the activity.

Developing the session

• Sing action songs and rhymes, such as 'Head, shoulders, knees and toes'.

• Ask the children to lie on the floor and move the different parts of the body named in turn.

• Ask the children to pair off. One child lies on the floor, face down, while the other gently touches the child, from head to toe, naming each part in turn. Then they change over.

• While still in pairs, each child lies down on a large sheet of paper while their partner draws an outline of them. The outlines are then cut out, named and the features drawn in.

• The children take the outline to the table and make patterns with paint, using fingers and hands.

• They clear away the paint and equipment and return to the chairs.

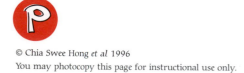

© Chia Swee Hong *et al* 1996
You may photocopy this page for instructional use only.

Closing the session

• Finish the session with action songs and rhymes with an adapted version of 'Head, shoulders, knees and toes':

'Head, arms and legs and toes, legs and toes,

Head, arms and legs and toes, legs and toes,

And hands and thumbs and ears and chin and nose,

Head, arms and legs and toes, legs and toes.'

© Chia Swee Hong *et al* 1996
You may photocopy this page for instructional use only.

SESSION 3

Aim:

Stimulating body awareness, encouraging movement and enhancing spatial awareness

Activity:

Body awareness 2

Materials:

Rug

Opening the session

- Sit behind the child and envelop him; rock him sideways rhythmically.

Developing the session

Ask the child to:

- sit facing a partner and hold hands and do a seesaw movement;
- lie on his side and to stiffen his body and roll as if he is a log, then to relax and roll smoothly;
- walk with knees stiff and bent;
- crawl on his stomach;
- lie on his stomach and spin on the floor;
- sit with knees bent up and pat and rub knees;
- curl up tightly and ask his partner to undo the 'parcel' he has made of himself.
- Ask groups of four children to line up side by side on hands and knees. One child lies across the back of the other children. If everyone is feeling confident, the kneeling children can crawl across the floor with the other child on their back.
- Staying in the same group, three children take up a position on their hands and knees to make a tunnel while the fourth child is encouraged to crawl through the tunnel.

© Chia Swee Hong *et al* 1996

You may photocopy this page for instructional use only.

- Ask one child to lie on a rug in a sleeping position. Hold either end of the rug so that the child is safely cradled and gently pull or lift the mat over the floor and gently swing it from side to side. Place another mat on the floor in case the child falls over.

- Everyone takes a turn to do each activity.

Closing the session

- The children let themselves fall to the ground with gradually bending knees, then lie and relax for a few minutes.

© Chia Swee Hong *et al* 1996
You may photocopy this page for instructional use only.

SESSION 4

Aim:

Stimulating sensory awareness and promoting hand skills

Activity:

Baking buns

Materials:

See ingredients

Opening the session

- Around the table, encourage each child to feel, smell, look at and taste a sample of the ingredients. **NB Do not taste raw egg.**

- You will require 75g margarine, 75g self-raising flour, 75g caster sugar, 1 large egg and 12 cake cases.

Developing the session

- Help each of the children in turn to weigh out one of the ingredients. Weigh some in smaller portions if there is not enough to go round.

- The children take turns at creaming butter and sugar, adding the beaten egg and folding in flour with a spoon. Make sure each child has a go and then passes the bowl to his neighbour.

- Help each child place a few cake cases in the tin and spoon the mixture in ready for baking.

- Place the tin on the middle shelf of a moderate oven.

- Many small cakes can be made using cereals and melted chocolate. Chocolate buttons can be melted in foil plates placed on hot water bottles.

Closing the session

- Have a mass wash-up/water play.

- Taste the finished product.

© Chia Swee Hong et al 1996
You may photocopy this page for instructional use only.

SESSION 5

Aim:
Stimulating sensory awareness and promoting hand skills

Activity:
Sand and water

Materials:
Trays, sand, water, containers for pouring etc

Opening the session

- Have trays — if possible, with dry sand and water. Have a spare tray or use one end of the dry sand tray to mix wet sand. Encourage the children to feel the sand and water, with their whole hands, if possible; some children will only be happy using their fingertips at first: encourage them to use their whole hands as they become more familiar with the activity.

Developing the session

- The children practise pouring, scooping and letting sand run between their fingertips, splashing, filling containers and burying objects to find again.

- They mix water into the sand and use the wet sand to make castles, drive cars through and poke holes in with fingers and thumbs.

- They try putting their bare feet into the trays.

Closing the session

- Everyone helps to take all the toys out of the sand and water.

- Make a game of finding them all and placing them in a storage container.

© Chia Swee Hong *et al* 1996
You may photocopy this page for instructional use only.

SESSION 6

Aim:

Stimulating sensory awareness and promoting hand skills

Activity:

Growing cress

Materials:

Cotton wool, egg shells, cress seeds, water

Opening the session

- Sit at a table. Explain the purpose of the session. Show an example. The children look at and hold the cress seeds, empty egg shells, cotton wool and water.

Developing the session

- The children put some cotton wool in the egg shells.
- They water the cotton wool so it is damp.
- They sprinkle the cress seeds on top.

Closing the session

- Tidy up.
- Keep the egg shells in a dark, warm place for a few days until the seeds sprout. Cut the cress, wash it and then eat it in a sandwich.

© Chia Swee Hong *et al* 1996
You may photocopy this page for instructional use only.

SESSION 7

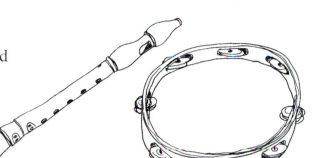

Aim:

Stimulating sensory awareness and promoting hand skills

Activity:

Music

Materials:

A collection of musical instruments (Winslow offer a Musical Instruments Box)

Opening session

• Pass a drum and sing. Beat the drum to the tune of 'The farmer in his den'.

• Pass a box of instruments around and ask each child to take one.

Developing the session

• Ask one child to play his instrument first and, after his turn, to request another child to play next.

• Establish a basic rhythm with one instrument — one by one, each child joins in with his instrument.

• Play all the instruments together. Start very softly, gradually getting louder and then fading away to nothing.

• Invite a child to 'conduct' by pointing to an individual child to start playing and by closing his fist to ask the others to stop.

Closing the session

• Everyone helps put the instruments away. Ask the children to clap hands slowly as they sing a closing song.

© Chia Swee Hong *et al* 1996
You may photocopy this page for instructional use only.

SESSION 8

Aim:

Stimulating sensory awareness and promoting hand skills

Activity:

Art

Materials:

Seeds, pulses, cardboard, glue, hole punch, strings

Opening the session

• Greet everyone and enquire how they are.

Developing the session

• The children are invited to unscrew some jars to look at and feel different kinds of seeds and pulses.

• Give a piece of cardboard to every child. An adult spreads glue on the board. The children choose seeds and pulses and sprinkle them on their boards.

• Spread glue on a large board and stick the individual boards onto it, (an adult should do this if the child is not able).

• Punch holes in the large board and thread round the edges with a shiny string, (this should be done by the children, with adult help if necessary).

Closing the session

• The children look at and feel the textured board. You could try a body or a face collage next time.

© Chia Swee Hong *et al* 1996
You may photocopy this page for instructional use only.

SESSION 9

Aim:

Promoting hand skills

Activity:

Making beads

Materials:

Coloured paper, knitting needles, glue, thin string, scissors

Opening the session

- Sit at a table. Lay out the materials. Show an example of a completed bead.

Developing the session

- The children cut the paper into strips.
- They paste the backs of the strips.
- They roll each strip firmly round a needle, press firmly, then take it off the needle and let it dry.

Closing the session

- The children thread the beads on a string and knot the ends of the string together if you are making a necklace or a bracelet.
- As well as making a necklace or a bracelet, the children could make a strip curtain, a toy snake or a spider with pipe-cleaner legs.

© Chia Swee Hong *et al* 1996
You may photocopy this page for instructional use only.

SESSION 10

Aim:

Encouraging basic movement and spatial awareness and promoting hand skills

Activity:

A bag of games

Materials:

Ball, various objects, such as a spoon, a mug, bricks, quoits and a parcel (containing nice rewards such as sweets)

Opening session

• Sit in a circle. Call out the name of a child and throw a ball to him; he will then throw it back to you.

• Go round the circle singing a 'hello' song, such as 'Hello, Sophie, hello Sophie. How are you? Very nice to see you, very nice to see you. How do you do?'

Developing the session

• 'Pass a squeeze', when every child has a turn to squeeze another child's hand.

• Clap hands. Ask a child to copy and add another movement: for example, clap hands and stamp feet.

• Put two objects, such as a spoon and a mug, into a bag. Ask the children to identify the objects. Add more objects, if appropriate.

• Ask a child to build a tower of five bricks. Seek permission from the child for the tower to be knocked down by another child. If this is given, invite another child to knock it down.

• Give a quoit to each child; they take turns to throw the quoits onto a cone.

• Pass the parcel — make sure everyone gets a go!

Closing the session

• Wave 'bye-bye'.

© Chia Swee Hong et al 1996
You may photocopy this page for instructional use only.

SESSION 11

Aim:

Encouraging basic movement and enhancing spatial awareness

Activity:

Obstacle course

Materials:

Bench, ladder, tunnel, small trampoline or mattress, ball, bean bags, space hopper

Opening the session

- Give each child a piece of equipment to start on and explain the direction of the circuit.

Developing the session

- Give each child time to experience and practise the movements required on each piece of equipment before moving on to the next. For example:

  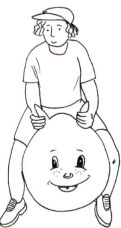

    bench — to pull along
    ladder — to step along
    tunnel — to crawl through
    small trampoline or mattress - to jump on
    ball - to throw at target
    beanbags - to balance on heads or arms
    while sitting and walking
    space hopper - to bounce on.

- To develop the session further, provide each child with a small bag and things to collect as they go round the course. For example, each child collects objects of a particular colour or a different animal.

Closing the session

- When everyone has completed all the obstacles, get together in the middle for a closing song or to look at the objects the children have collected.

© Chia Swee Hong *et al* 1996
You may photocopy this page for instructional use only.

SESSION 12

Aim:

Encouraging basic movement and enhancing spatial awareness

Activity:

Movement

Materials:

None needed

Opening the session

- Give the children the following instructions. Move anywhere in the room. Continue to move round the room and when you see a space, go to it and remain still for one or two seconds. Move again. If you can jump — jump as high as you can. Try coming down as low as you can.

Developing the session

- The children move and spin on the spot, finishing high at first and low later.
- They move with their hands and feet on the floor, taking up a little space and then a lot of space.
- Can they find another way of moving, this time with their bodies on the floor?
- They stretch on the floor and then curl up. Now they have to find another way of stretching out.
- They curl up in a little ball on the floor and roll along.
- They stretch their bodies and roll along.

Closing the session

- The children roll to a comfortable space. They lie on their backs and relax each part of their body, starting from their feet.

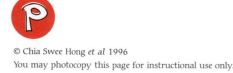

© Chia Swee Hong *et al* 1996
You may photocopy this page for instructional use only.

SESSION 13

Aim:

Encouraging basic movement and stimulating sensory awareness

Activity:

Exploring texture: spiky and smooth

Materials:

None needed

Opening the session

- Ask the children to imagine that they are spiky and to try to dance with different parts of their bodies.

Developing the session

Give the children the following instructions:

- Make your hands into a spiky shape. Dance with spiky hands. Imagine they are smooth. Dance with smooth hands.

- Make your feet spiky. Dance with spiky feet. Imagine they are now smooth. Dance with smooth feet.

- Dance with spiky hands and feet and then dance with smooth hands and feet.

- Imagine you are attending the grand ball at the Palace of The Snow Queen. Dance with your spiky body, hands and feet. Try and dance later with smooth hands, feet and body.

Closing the session

- The children find a place on the floor they feel comfortable in and imagine they are melting away.

© Chia Swee Hong *et al* 1996
You may photocopy this page for instructional use only.

SESSION 14

Aim:

Encouraging basic movement and spatial awareness and stimulating sensory awareness

Activity:

Drama

Materials:

None needed

Opening the session

- Sit in a circle. Call out the name of a child, who will shake hands with you.

Developing the session

- Encourage children to mime: for example, picking fruit, wiping the table or sweeping the floor.

- Work in pairs — one child massages the arms and hands of another child. Take turns to do this.

- Work in pairs — partners touch hands and move together gently, mirroring the movement.

- Divide the group into two; ask one group to blow the other as if they are a large balloon. Burst it.

Closing the session

- The children sit in a large circle, close their eyes and link hands. They breathe in and out gently. They concentrate on breathing.

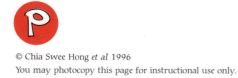

© Chia Swee Hong *et al* 1996
You may photocopy this page for instructional use only.

SESSION 15

Aim:

Encouraging basic movement and spatial awareness

Activity:

Parachute games

Materials:

Parachute (or a large bed sheet)

Opening the session

- Say 'hello' to all the children and explain the nature of the activity.

Developing the session

- The children sit or stand around the parachute. Ask them to hold it tightly, and wave it gently.
- Put a ball in the parachute. Encourage the children to hold the parachute and bounce the ball.
- The children roll the ball around by raising and lowering their arms alternately, forming a wave effect.
- Ask two children to be a mouse and a cat. The mouse lives under the parachute and the cat on top of the parachute. Ask the cat to catch the mouse, and ask the other children holding the parachute to make a lot of different noises to distract the cat.
- Ask the children to lie on the floor. If possible, get two adults to wave the parachute and let it fall gently on the children.

Closing the session

- Ask the children to sit in a circle and hold the parachute. They wave it gently while singing an appropriate closing down song.

© Chia Swee Hong *et al* 1996
You may photocopy this page for instructional use only.

7

More creative ideas

Little Sally Saucer

Sitting in the water

Rise Sally Rise

Wipe your eyes

Turn to the east star

Turn to the west star

Point to the one you like best

At the outset, our aim was to help carers and newly qualified practitioners who asked the question, "Where do I begin?". Having identified aims and started a programme of activities with your child, the next hurdle will be to provide a variety of activities and games to maintain the child's interest, motivation and progress.

In this chapter, we have started an alphabetical resource list, with aims followed by our tried and tested techniques and ideas. Working around a theme may help you to develop more ideas and activities.

Animals

Stimulating sensory and body awareness

Listen to and try to copy noises made by animals.
Visit zoos, farms or watch other people's pets.
Smell different animals eg. horses.
Stroke different animals such as tortoises, cows and sheep.

Encouraging basic movement

Try horse riding.
Walk the dog.
Pretend to move eg. swim like a fish.

Promoting hand skills

Use flat hands to stroke animals.
Use different grasps to handle small or large toy animals.
Place animals into containers.
Make toy animals 'walk' in pretend play.
Hold on to a dog's lead.

Enhancing spatial and early perceptual awareness

Sort animals into groups eg. pigs, sheep, cows and dogs.
Sort little and big animals.
Find pictures of animals which are doing different things — cows standing/cows lying down for instance.

Balls

Stimulating sensory and body awareness

Play with balls with bells in, or use different textured balls or those which glow in the dark, light up or reflect light.
Roll a ball slowly from left to right so that your child can follow it with his eyes. Make it disappear behind your back and wait for eye contact. When playing games, wait for your child to look at you before, for example, rolling the ball to him.

Encouraging basic movement

Hold large beach balls.
Throw or catch with one or two hands.
Sit on a very large ball or space hopper and bounce up and down.
Kick balls of varying sizes.

Promoting hand skills

Throw at a target.
Grasp balls of different sizes.
Release balls of varying sizes into large and small containers.
Hit a suspended ball with a bat.

Enhancing spatial and early perceptual awareness

Sort and match games using balls.
Arrange balls in order of size.
Match different size balls to an appropriate sized container.

Clothing

Stimulating sensory and body awareness

Feel different textured clothing.
Encourage awareness of the part of the body the piece of clothing is for.

Encouraging basic movement

Clap with gloves on.
Jump in wellies.

Promoting hand skills

Use zips, buttons and other fasteners.
Use crayons or colour pencils to draw pictures of clothing eg. different types of clothing for various weather conditions.

Enhancing spatial and early perceptual awareness

Try on little and big clothes, hats, socks and shoes (see Figure 14).
Play with puzzles of people which then have the clothes placed on in another layer.
Dress up dolls.
Take out a variety of clothes and talk about which are suitable for which kinds of weather.

Figure 14 *Putting on a T-shirt*

Colours

Stimulating sensory and body awareness

Use bath crayons to colour different parts of the body and then wash off.
Try finger painting or foot painting with different colours.

Encouraging basic movement

Place different coloured mats on the floor. Step from one to the other — name the colours.
Move in different ways - jump, hop or skip.

Promoting hand skills

Play with colour matching puzzles and games.
Play with board games using coloured dice.
Put coloured spots on fingers.

Enhancing spatial and early perceptual awareness

Find all the objects with a specific colour, eg. red, in a room.
Match objects of the same colour ie. red wellies, black wellies and green wellies.
Does your child know the names of the basic colours? Can he match colours as in Figure 15?

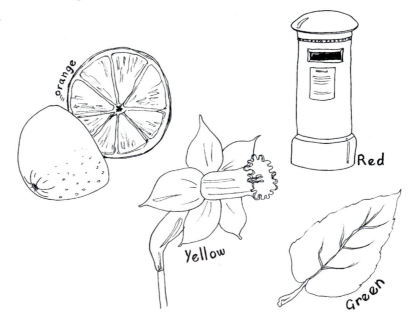

Figure 15 *Can you find things in your house that are the same colour as these things?*

Copying

Stimulating sensory and body awareness

The adult makes funny faces in the mirror and the child copies.

Have a set of objects you can use: for example, bang two bricks, shake a handbell, squeeze a toy and push a toy car. Ask your child to copy your actions.

Encouraging basic movement

Play 'Simon Says': wash your feet, put your finger on your nose, open and close your fist, drum your hands on the table, and so on. Walk in different ways.

Play follow my leader — the leader performs different actions for the others to copy or uses a soft toy such as a rabbit to perform different activities, again to copy.

Promoting hand skills

Copy action songs and finger rhymes.

Give your child the opportunity to copy everyday activities around the house, such as dusting, washing, cooking and sweeping.

Enhancing spatial and early perceptual awareness

Copy movements using a doll — eg. you lift your arms above your head, then ask the child to make dolly do the same.

In a Wendy house, have two cups, two teddy bears and two pairs of sunglasses. Copy your child's play. For example, if he puts on sunglasses, you do the same. See if your child copies your actions.

Cornflour

Encouraging sensory and body awareness

Try this recipe for Magic Cornflour (you will need some cornflour, a large bowl and a small jug of water). Put the cornflour in a large bowl with sufficient water to produce a thick consistency. Let it all settle in the bowl. Take some of the mixture in your hand — it is solid but will slide away through your fingers in a few minutes. Mix cornflour paste (1 cup cornflour, 1 cup cold water, 1 cup boiling water. Dissolve the cornflour in the cold water. Add the boiling water and stir quickly to reduce lumps). Play with the paste using hands and feet and use it later for *papier mâché*.

Encouraging basic movement

Make big movements with arms, small movements with fingertips in a large tray of cornflour powder or 'gloop', (make with one packet of cornflour, ½ pint [slightly less than one litre] of water and different food colourings). You will also need plastic mixing bowls, aprons and paper to cover the floor and table tops. Put the cornflour in a bowl. Add most of the water. Mix, adding more water until the gloop feels sticky and slimy. Add food colouring gradually until you get the colour you want. Test the texture by putting some on a spoon; it should harden slightly and go gloopy! Use gloop drips to make patterns. Put some gloop on the floor and sit and wiggle your toes in it.

Promoting hand skills

Let powder run between thumb and finger ends.
Poke fingers and thumb into cornflour paste.

Enhancing spatial and early perceptual awareness

Hide objects/shapes in the cornflour and try to identify them by touch.
Draw patterns on cornflour paste.

Do it yourself (or adapted) games

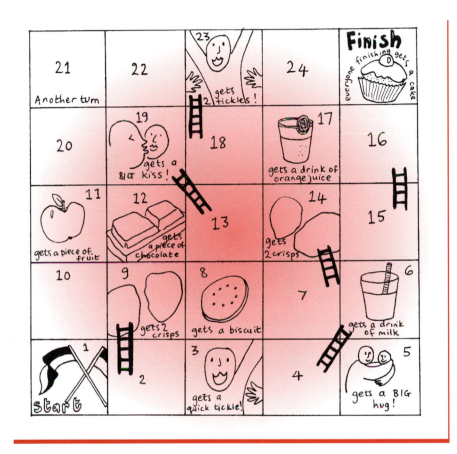

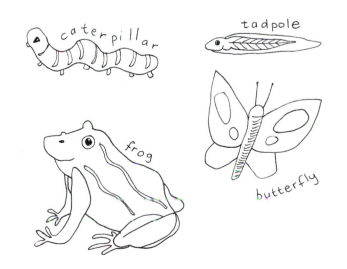

Figure 16 *Can you match these baby animals with what they will look like when they grow up?*

Figure 17 *Which go together?*

Empty containers such as margarine tubs

Stimulating sensory and body awareness

Fill the tubs with different materials, seal the lid and use them as shakers.
Put liquids, bricks, sand and so on in the tubs.

Encouraging basic movement

Use large tubs as shoes!
Use tubs as obstacles to step over, walk round.

Promoting hand skills

Put different things inside the tubs.
Use tubs for printing.
Fill different sized tubs with various materials to make them heavy/light.

Enhancing spatial and early perceptual awareness

Grade tubs in size.
Use tubs to make shapes.
Use tubs for sorting, matching and counting.

Opposites

Stimulating sensory and body awareness

Make loud and soft noises.
Rub different textures ie. smooth and rough, on various parts of the body.
Play with warm and cold water.
Go in to dark and bright rooms.

Encouraging basic movement

Use big and small steps.
Create high and low obstacles.
Get in and out of large boxes.
Go on top and under tunnels or tables.

Promoting hand skills

Grasp large and small objects.
Grasp light and heavy objects.

Enhancing spatial and early perceptual awareness

Choose pictures which show opposites eg. young and old, big and small, thin and fat, long and short, left and right, front and back, up and down, happy and sad, narrow and wide, hot and cold, push and pull, open and shut and materials which are dry and wet, soft and hard, light and heavy, quiet and noisy. Ask your child to say which is which.

Seasonal activities (eg. Easter)

Stimulating sensory and body awareness

Taste eggs — boiled, scrambled, chocolate! Feel the shape of different kinds of eggs. Stroke rabbits. Sing Easter songs — 'Hot Cross Buns' and so on.

Encouraging basic movement

Sing 'Hot Cross Buns' and roll along a mat to collect buns at one end and deliver them at the other.
Play shopping games — for eggs, hot cross buns and so on.

Promoting hand skills

Decorate egg shapes with hand or footprints.
Make *Playdough* eggs and put in egg boxes.

Enhancing spatial and early perceptual awareness

Organize an obstacle 'egg hunt' course so that the child has to climb over a wedge or crawl under a tunnel constructed from soft play bricks to get the egg.

Shapes

Stimulating sensory and body awareness

Look at and feel shapes of different objects around school and home.
Identify an object by touch, hide it in a bag and then ask the child to feel it and say what it is.
Identify shapes out of a shape puzzle by touch.

Encouraging basic movement

Make shapes with pieces of carpet or paper (circle, square, triangle, oblong), lay them on the floor and ask the child to stand on a circle, square and so on.
Ask the child to walk around the shape.
Ask the child to 'walk' the shape without the carpet or paper template.

Promoting hand skills

Play with shape puzzles.
Thread different shaped beads.
Draw around shape templates, colouring in and cutting them out.

Enhancing spatial and early perceptual awareness

Copy designs using different shapes.
Make a set of Snap cards using shapes (square, circle, triangle, oblong, diamond and star) and colours. Play the game.
Sequence a simple pattern eg. circle, square. Progress to more complex sequences.

Figure 18 *Can you find all the shapes in the picture?*

Sizes: Big and Little

Stimulating sensory and body awareness

Look at big and little objects around the house eg. clothes, cutlery.

Encouraging basic movement

Make big steps when walking along then change to little steps.
Climb up on to a big box or table, stand on a little box or step.
Stand up and stretch really tall then crouch down and make yourself very small.
Sing... "Jack in the box, small as a mouse, deep down inside your little dark house. Jack in the box, ever so still, will you come out? Yes, I will".

Promoting hand skills

Make big movements involving the whole arm eg. drawing big circles in sand.
Make small movements using hand or index finger only eg. drawing small circles in sand.
Play with big and small balls and bricks.

Enhancing spatial and early perceptual awareness

Match games using big and little 'Snap' cards or big and little lotto.
Put together nesting toys or graded rings on a stick.
Try on big clothes and shoes; compare with little clothes and shoes.

Skipping ropes

Stimulating sensory and body awareness

Encourage the child to lay on the floor, lay the rope round the edge of his body, then ask him to stand up and look at the outline. Repeat with the child laying the rope around your body.

Encouraging basic movement

Jump over the rope laid on the ground in different ways eg. bunny hops, jumping both feet together.
Jump forwards, backwards, sideways.
Walk balancing on the rope laid on the floor.

Promoting hand skills

Hold one end of the rope and see what patterns can be made moving it up and down, side to side or round in a circle. Play tug-o-war

Enhancing spatial and early perceptual awareness

Lay the rope around the house; the child has to follow the rope road to reach a reward.
Lay the rope around various obstacles on the floor.
Ask the child to follow visually the direction the rope takes and name the obstacles it passes in order to get a reward.

Stories

Use popular stories such as 'Goldilocks and the Three Bears': Once upon a time there were three bears. They lived in a cottage in the forest. There was Father Bear, Mother Bear and Baby Bear. One day Goldilocks went into the bears' kitchen, where she saw three bowls of porridge on the table. She tried the porridge in the big bowl, but it was too sweet. She tried the porridge in the medium-sized bowl, but that was too salty. She tried the porridge in the smallest bowl. That was just right. She ate it all up...

Stimulating sensory and body awareness

Look at the pictures of the bowls and introduce the concept of taste.
Try different tastes — sweet and salty porridge.
Lay on hard/soft surfaces.
Make noises like bears.
Feel furry materials.

Encouraging basic movement

Ask your child to be a bear, walking on all four limbs to the forest.

Promoting hand skills

Tell the story using gestures, Makaton signs or other signs along with the nursery rhyme.

Enhancing spatial and perceptual skills

Match big, medium and small bears, plates, spoons, chairs and beds.
Sequence each of the above.

The Community

Stimulating sensory and body awareness

Visit markets, libraries or places of interest.
Watch the seasons.
Explore sensory gardens.
When out and about, observe the seasons — watch ants around an ants' nest, birds feeding or clouds moving across the sky. Look at and talk about the flowers, hanging baskets and fountains. Collect leaves and shells. Visit take-aways or restaurants to taste different foods.

Figure 19 *Can you find the things that go with each season?*

Encouraging basic movement

Explore adventure playgrounds, shops with escalators, stairs, lifts, revolving doors, swimming pools, ball pools and soft play areas.
Point out things you see. Let the child feel them, if appropriate.
Go for walks with crisp autumn leaves under foot.
Listen to traffic on the road as it goes through a tunnel.

Promoting hand skills

Play with pretend money — place it in containers.
Make *Playdough* food.
Play at libraries — stamping tickets and putting cards in books.

Enhancing spatial and early perceptual awareness

Ask your child to lead you to the local shop, playgroup or library.
As he gets older, see if he can tell you how to get there.

Transport

Stimulating sensory and body awareness

Listen to traffic, such as trains or cars, going by.
Visit airports and railway stations.
Travel by bus or train if you can.

Encouraging basic movement

Play at trains, stepping along a ladder laid on the floor.
Pretend to be cars following a road laid on the floor, avoiding obstacles.

Promoting hand skills

Push cars along the floor, moving arm and hand right across the body.
Place 'men' in toy cars eg. *Duplo*®, *Playmobil*® or little wooden cars.

Enhancing spatial and early perceptual awareness

Encourage your child to make a line of cars from left to right, then to put them away in the 'garage' one at a time from left to right.

Bibliography

Addison R, *Bright Ideas for Early Years: Music*, Scholastic Publications, Leamington Spa, 1987.

Britton L, *Montessori Play and Learn*, Vermillion, London, 1992.

Campbell J, *Creative Art in Groupwork*, Speechmark Publishing, Bicester, 1993.

Carter M, *Nursery Treasury Chest*, Kingfisher Books, London, 1991.

Cooke J, *Early Sensory Skills*, Speechmark Publishing, Bicester, 1996.

Cunliffe J & Ganeri A, *Round the Year with Rosie and Jim*, Scholastic Children's Books, London, 1992.

Dale FJ, *The Stimulation Guide*, Woodhead Faulkner, Cambridge, 1990.

De Boo M, *Bright Ideas for Early Years: Action Rhymes and Games*, Scholastic Publications, Leamington Spa, 1992.

Denziloe J, *Fun and Games – Practical Leisure Ideas for People with Profound Disabilities*, Butterworth-Heinemann, Oxford, 1994.

Dunn ML, *Pre-Scissor Skills*, Communication Skill Builders, Tucson, Arizona, 1979.

Dynes R, *Creative Games in Groupwork*, Speechmark Publishing, Bicester, 1990.

Fawdrey J & Jackson B, *Creative Ideas*, Speechmark Publishing, Bicester, 1986.

Fink B, *Sensory Motor Integration Activities*, Therapy Skill Builders, Tucson, Arizona, 1989.

Finnie N, *Handling the Young Cerebral Palsied Child at Home*, Heinemann, Oxford, 1990.

Golding R & Goldsmith L, *The Caring Person's Guide to Handling the Severely Multiple Handicapped*, Macmillan Education, Basingstoke, 1986.

Health Education Authority, *Birth to Five*, Health Education Authority, London, 1990.

Heggie A, *Bright Ideas for Early Years: Art & Craft*, Scholastic Publications, Leamington Spa, 1989.

Jennings S, *Creative Drama in Groupwork*, Speechmark Publishing, Bicester, 1986.

Klein MD, *Pre-Writing Skills*, Communication Skill Builders, Tucson, Arizona, 1982.

Klein MD, *Pre-Dressing Skills*, Communication Skill Builders, Tucson, Arizona, 1983.

Knill M & Knill C, *Activity Programmes for Body Awareness*, Contact & Communication, LDA, Wisbech, 1986.

LadyBird, *Learning at Home – ABC*, *Colours and Shapes*, *First Counting*, *Tell the Time*, *Begin to Write Book 1*, *Begin to Write Book 2*, LadyBird Books, Leicester, 1993.

Lear R, *More Play Helps*, Butterworth-Heinemann, Oxford, 1990 (revised edition).

Lear R, *Play Helps*, Butterworth-Heinemann, Oxford, 1993.

Levitt S, *Basic Motor Abilities – A Whole Approach*, Souvenir Press, London, 1994.

Levitt S, *Treatment of Cerebral Palsy and Motor Delay*, Blackwell Science, Oxford, 1995.

Longhorn F, *A Sensory Curriculum for Very Special People*, Souvenir Press, London, 1988.

Lynch C & Cooper J, *Early Communication Skills*, Speechmark Publishing/Winslow Press, Bicester, 1991.

Mackay GF & Dunn WR, *Early Communicative Skills*, Routledge, London, 1989.

Marshall R, *My Cook Book*, British Institute of Learning Disabilities, Kidderminster, 1992.

Masheder M, *Let's Cooperate*, Play for Life, Norwich, 1989.

Matterson E, *This Little Puffin Nursery Songs and Rhymes*, Penguin Books, Harmondsworth, 1991.

Mencap, *Leisure Resource Pack*, MENCAP PIMD, Manchester, 1991.

Morris J & Mort L, *Bright Ideas for Early Years: Learning Through Play*, Scholastic Publications, Leamington Spa, 1990.

Mort L & Morris J, *Bright Ideas for Early Years: Starting with Rhyme*, Scholastic Publications, Leamington Spa, 1991.

Norris D, *Have You Tried? A Handbook of Activities and Services for People with Profound Learning Disabilities*, Costello, London, 1988.

Ouvry C & Mitchell S, *Make It Simple*, The Consortium, London, 1990.

Payne H, *Creative Movement and Dance in Groupwork*, Speechmark Publishing, Bicester, 1990.

Peck C & Hong CS, *Living Skills for Mentally Handicapped People*, Chapman & Hall, London, 1994.

Pointer B, *Movement Activities for Children with Learning Difficulties*, Jessica Kingsley, London, 1993.

Presland J, *Paths To Mobility*, British Institute of Mental Handicap, Kidderminster, 1982.

Roberts S, *PlaySongs – Action Songs and Rhymes for Babies and Toddlers* (plus a C40 cassette), PlaySong Publications, London, 1991.

Russell JP, *Graded Activities for Children with Motor Difficulties*, Cambridge University Press, Cambridge, 1988.

Sanderson H, Harrison J & Price S, *Aromatherapy and Massage for People with Learning Difficulties*, Hand On Publishing, Birmingham, 1991.

Sherborne V, *Developmental Movement for Children*, Cambridge University Press, Cambridge, 1990.

White M, Bungay C & Gabriel H, *Guide to Early Movement Skills*, NFER–Nelson, Windsor, 1994.

Whiteford R & Fitzsimmons J, *Bright Ideas for Early Years: Music & Movement*, Scholastic Publications, Leamington Spa, 1991.

Williams D, *Early Listening Skills*, Speechmark Publishing, Bicester, 1995.

Wood J, *My First Bear Book and My Second Bear Book*, Liber Press, Oxford, 1992.

Wood M, *Music for Mentally Handicapped People*, Souvenir Press, London, 1983.

Useful Organizations

United Kingdom

Active
68 Churchway
London NW1 1LT

Association of Paediatric Chartered Physiotherapists
c/o Chartered Society of Physiotherapy
14 Bedford Row
London WC1R 4ED
Website: www.csp.org.uk

Council for Disabled Children
8 Wakley Street
London WC1V 7QE
Website: www.ncb.org.uk

Disabled Living Foundation
380–384 Harrow Road
London W9 2HU
Website: www.dlf.org.uk

National Association for Special Education Needs
York House
Exhall Grange
Wheelwright Lane
Coventry CV7 9HP

National Association of Paediatric Occupational Therapists (NAPOT)
65 Prestbury Road
Wilmslow
Cheshire SK9 2LL
Email: htidey@napot.u-net.com

National Association of Toy and Leisure Libraries
68 Churchway
London NW1 1LT
Website: www.natll.org.uk

Occupational Therapists — Special Interest Group — Learning Disabilities
c/o College of Occupational Therapists
6–8 Marshalsea Road
London SE1 1HL

Planet
Cambridge House
Cambridge Grove
London W6 0LE

PlayTrac
Horizon Trust
Harperbury
Harper Lane
Radlett
Herts WD7 9HQ

Pre-School Playgroup Association
61–63 Kings Cross Road
London WC1X 9LL

Royal College of Speech and Language Therapists
2/3 White Hart Yard
London SE1 1NX
Tel: 0207 378 1200
Website: www.rcslt.org

United States of America

Active 20–30 International
1915 I Street
Sacramento
California 95814
Website: www.active20-30.com

American Physical Therapy Association
111 North Fairfax Street
Alexandria
Virginia 22314
Website: www.apta.org

American Disability Association
2201 Sixth Avenue South
Birmingham
Alabama 35233
Website: www.adanet.org

National Organization on Disability
910 Sixteenth Street NW #600
Washington, DC 20006
Website: www.nod.org

American Occupational Therapy Association
4720 Montgomery Lane
PO Box 31220
Bethesda
Maryland 20824-1220
Website: www.aota.org

The Council for Exceptional Children
1110 North Glebe Road, Suite 300
Arlington
Virginia 22201-5704
Website: www.cec.sped.org

Association for Children and Adults with Learning Disabilities
4156 Library Road
Pittsburgh
Pennsylvania 15234

Association for Play Therapy Inc
2050 N Winery Ave, Suite 101
Fresno
California 93703
Website: www.iapt.org

American Speech–Language–Hearing Association
10801 Rockville Pike
Rockville
Maryland 20852
Website: www.asha.org
Note: All states have state speech–language–hearing associations

Early Skills ... the Complete Series

In dealing with day-to-day management of clients, the Speechmark Early Skills . . . series has established an enviable reputation as the essential resource for every speech and language professional. The following titles are available:

Early Sensory Skills
Jackie Cooke

A compendium of practical and enjoyable activities for vision, touch, taste and smell. Invaluable to anyone working with young children, this text outlines major principles and aims followed by six easy-to-use sections containing basic activities, everyday activities, games and topics to stimulate the senses.

Early Movement Skills
Naomi Benari

This fifth title in Speechmark's *Early Skills* series is designed to help anyone caring for very young children, whether in home, school or clinic. With graded activities, it encourages the use of movement to enhance cognitive, emotional and physical development.

Related Resources
Storycards: Verbs, Prepositions, Adjectives
Sue Duggleby & Ross Duggleby
A new approach to learning basic language concepts.
Social Skills Programmes
Maureen Aarons & Tessa Gittens
An integrated approach from early years to adolescence
Pocket ColorCards®
The world's leading photographic language cards

Early Visual Skills
Diana Williams

This recent addition to the *Early Skills* series is intended for use by professionals who are working with children who have under-developed visual perceptual skills associated with language delay or other communication difficulties. It is a practical manual offering photocopiable activities designed to stimulate and develop visual attention and discrimination skills.

Early Listening Skills
Diana Williams

Early Listening Skills is a highly practical, comprehensive and effective manual for professionals working with pre-school children or the older special needs child. It contains more than 200 activities, all of which can be photocopied.

Early Communication Skills
Charlotte Lynch & Julia Kidd

In this new revised edition of one of the most popular titles in the *Early Skills* series, the authors have updated and revised their educational and therapeutic ideas for work with pre-school children and their families.

These are just a few of the many therapy resources available from Speechmark. A free catalogue will be sent on request. For further information please contact: